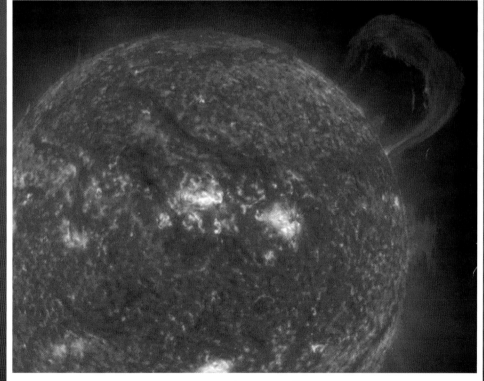

OUR GALAXY AND BEYOND

THE SUN

By Darlene R. Stille

THE CHILD'S WORLD®
CHANHASSEN, MINNESOTA

The Child's World

Published in the United States of America by The Child's World®
P.O. Box 326, Chanhassen, MN 55317-0326
800-599-READ
www.childsworld.com

Content Adviser:
Michelle Nichols,
Lead Educator for
Informal Programs,
Adler Planetarium
& Astronomy
Museum, Chicago,
Illinois

Photo Credits: Cover: NASA/JPL/Caltech/SOHO; AFP/Corbis: 20, 26; Bettmann/
Corbis: 8, 17; Corbis: 5 (Archivo Iconografico, S. A.), 6 (NASA), 24; NASA: 7
(SOHO), 9 (ESA), 15 (ISAS), 25 (N. Walborn and J. Ma`iz-Apell`aniz Space
Telescope Science Institute, R. Barb`a La Plata, Argentina), 27 (JPL/Caltech/Space
Telescope Science Institute), 31 (JPL/Caltech); NASA/Marshall Space Flight Center:
11 (David Hathaway), 12, 16, 21, 23 (Royal Swedish Academy of Science/Lockheed
Martin Solar and Astrophysics Laboratory); Royal Swedish Academy of Science: 19;
UCAR/NCAR/High Altitude Observatory: 13, 22.

The Child's World®: Mary Berendes, Publishing Director
Editorial Directions, Inc.: E. Russell Primm, Editorial Director; Dana Rau, Line
Editor; Elizabeth K. Martin, Assistant Editor; Olivia Nellums, Editorial Assistant;
Susan Hindman, Copy Editor; Susan Ashley, Proofreader; Kevin Cunningham,
Peter Garnham, Chris Simms, Fact Checkers; Tim Griffin/IndexServ, Indexer;
Cian Loughlin O'Day, Photo Researcher; Linda S. Koutris, Photo Selector

Library of Congress Cataloging-in-Publication Data
Stille, Darlene R.
 The sun / by Darlene Stille.
    p. cm. — (Our galaxy and beyond)
Summary: Introduces the sun, exploring its atmosphere, composition, and other
characteristics and looking particularly at how humans learned about the star at
the center of our solar system. Includes bibliographical references and index.
 ISBN 1-59296-055-3 (lib. bdg. : alk. paper)
 1. Sun—Juvenile literature. [1. Sun.] I. Title. II. Series.
 QB521.5.S844 2004
 523.7—dc21   2003006336

TABLE OF CONTENTS

CHAPTER ONE

4 Discovering the Sun

CHAPTER TWO

9 Inside the Sun

CHAPTER THREE

13 The Sun's Atmosphere

CHAPTER FOUR

17 Sunspots

CHAPTER FIVE

21 Solar Storms

CHAPTER SIX

25 The Birth and Death of the Sun

28 Glossary

28 Did You Know?

29 Fast Facts

30 How to Learn More about the Sun

32 Index

DISCOVERING THE SUN

The Sun is important to all life on Earth. People have always thought that there was something very special about the Sun. Some ancient people thought the Sun was a god. They believed that the Sun was the giver of all life. They worshiped the Sun.

Today, we know that the Sun is a star, a huge glowing ball of gas. The Sun is also the biggest object in our solar system. All nine planets in our solar system orbit, or go around, the Sun, which spins in the center of the solar system. The Sun itself orbits the center of our galaxy, the Milky Way. A galaxy is a huge group of stars, planets, gas, and dust held together by forces of **gravity.** The Milky Way is made up of more than one trillion stars. It takes the Sun about 200 million years to orbit the center of the Milky Way. It travels in its orbit at about 150 miles (241 kilo-

meters) per second.

The Sun is the closest

star to Earth. It is the

source of most energy on

Earth. The Sun's heat makes

Earth warm enough for living

Many ancient civilizations, including the Egyptians, looked up to the Sun as an important god. This Egyptian relief shows the people making offerings to the Sun.

things. Plants use the energy from sunlight to make food. They also

give off oxygen. Animals get energy from breathing oxygen and eat-

ing plants. People eat those plants and animals for food energy.

The Sun looks like it moves because Earth is always turning on

its axis. An axis is an imaginary line going through a planet from the

top to the bottom. Earth completes one turn every 24 hours.

Different parts of Earth face the Sun at different times of the day.

Every day the Sun seems to rise and set, but this is only because of Earth's rotation.

This makes the Sun look as if it is moving across the sky or rising

and setting. It is daytime on the side of Earth facing the Sun. On

the side of Earth facing away from the Sun, it is nighttime.

It was hard for ancient people to study the Sun. They could

not look directly at the Sun because light from the Sun can harm

people's eyes. Over time, **astronomers** have learned how to

put special cameras on their **telescopes** to take pictures of the

Sun. Today, astronomers also

study light given off by the

Sun. The light can tell them

what the Sun is made of.

They use instruments on a

robot spacecraft called the

Solar and Heliospheric

Observatory, or *SOHO,* to

study the Sun. Every day,

they learn more about the

Sun and its importance.

Many engineers worked on the construction of the SOHO spacecraft.

Many ancient people believed the Sun was a god. Some cultures thought that an eclipse meant the god was angry. An eclipse is caused by the Moon passing between Earth and the Sun. From Earth, it looks like the Sun has gone dark. These ancient people made offerings to the angry Sun god.

They also tried to explain how the Sun moves across the sky. The ancient Egyptians thought the Sun god sailed a boat across the sky. The ancient Greeks thought the Sun god drove a chariot. They called the Sun Helios. The ancient Romans called it Sol.

The Inca and Maya used the movement of the Sun to make calendars. They remembered where the Sun was in the sky at different times of the year. They used this knowledge to tell them when to plant crops. Many ancient people used the Sun to tell time. The Babylonians invented a sundial 4,000 years ago to show the hours of a day. The Sun cast a shadow on the dial as it seemed to move across the sky.

CHAPTER TWO

INSIDE THE SUN

The Sun has several layers. Each layer is made of gas, mostly

hydrogen and helium. About 75 percent of the Sun is made of

hydrogen gas. About 25 percent is made of helium. Deep inside

*This dramatic photo uses color in a special way so that
scientists can see some of the Sun's many layers.*

the Sun is the core, or the center. It is hotter than we can imagine, about 28 million degrees Fahrenheit (16 million degrees Celsius)!

The Sun's core makes all its energy. The heat that you feel and the light that you see from the Sun started in its core. But that energy has to go through the different layers of the Sun to get to us on Earth. Energy from the core is so hot that it must travel as light rays. When the core lets out energy as rays of light, it is called radiation. The energy travels out from the core through the radiation zone. It takes millions of years for energy to pass through this zone.

Outside of the radiation zone is an area called the convection zone. This zone is cooler than the radiation zone. The Sun's energy can travel through the convection zone as heat instead of light rays. Hot gases bubble and swirl in the convection zone the way water boils in a pot. Sometimes, bubbles of hot gas burst through to the surface of the Sun.

The surface of the Sun is called the photosphere. The photosphere is not solid like Earth's surface. Instead, it is made of hot

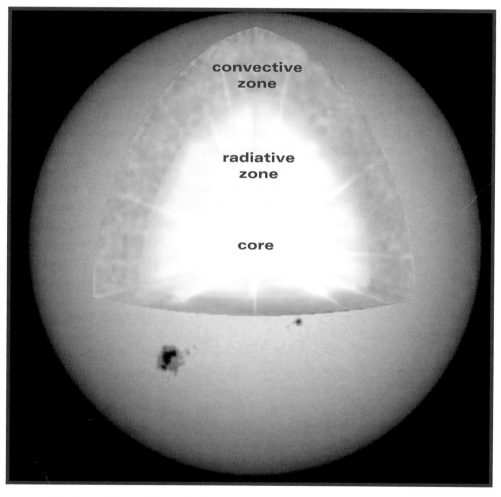

It takes millions of years for the Sun's heat to move from the deepest interior of the core out through its different layers to shed light on Earth.

The hot gas that makes up the Sun's photosphere, or surface layer,
is about 60 miles (96.5 km) thick.

gas. After the Sun's energy gets to the photosphere, it goes out into

space as heat and light. We feel the Sun's heat and see it shining

because of the energy that reaches the photosphere.

CHAPTER THREE

THE SUN'S ATMOSPHERE

Astronomers also call the photosphere the bottom layer of the Sun's atmosphere. An atmosphere is the layer of gases that surrounds a planet or another object. The outer layers of helium and hydrogen gas

The chromosphere and other parts of the Sun's atmosphere can only be seen using special techniques. Temperatures in the chromosphere range between 10,858° F (6,000° C) to 36,058° F (20,000° C).

form the Sun's atmosphere. The chromosphere is the next layer of the Sun's atmosphere. This layer is made of hot, swirling gases.

The top layer of the Sun's atmosphere is called the corona. The corona is very hot. Astronomers think the temperature of the corona is about 4 million degrees F (2.2 million degrees C). The chromosphere is actually cooler than the corona, even though it is closer to the center of the Sun. The temperature in the chromosphere is only about 50,000° F (27,800° C). Astronomers do not know why the corona is so much hotter.

Astronomers can study the corona with the help of spacecraft such as *SOHO*. They can also see the corona from Earth during an eclipse. During an eclipse, the Moon seems to cover the main part of the Sun. The Sun looks like a dark circle with a ring of white light around it. That ring of light is the Sun's corona.

The gases of the corona thin out more as they get farther from the Sun. Gases at the edge of the corona go off into space. These gases are called the solar wind.

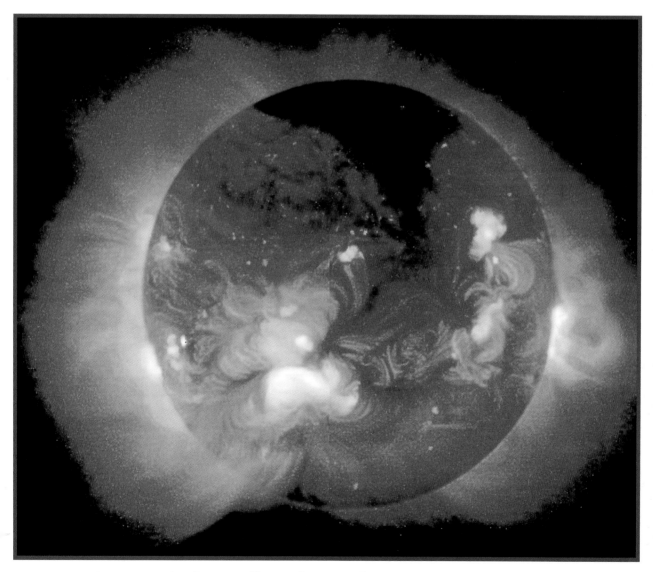

Astronomers take advantage of lunar eclipses to study the immensely hot corona of the Sun.

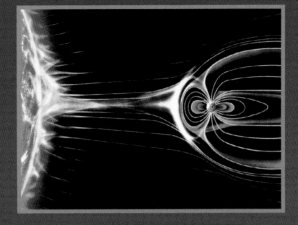

The solar wind is not like wind on Earth. Earth's wind is moving air. The solar wind is made of gas. It "blows" out of the Sun's corona and streams off into space, going past all the planets.

The solar wind travels through space at speeds from 155 to 625 miles (250 to 1,000 km) per second. Sometimes it passes a comet. It pushes material away from the comet to add to its tail. Sometimes the solar wind passes a planet with a magnetic field around it. A magnetic field is the area where a magnet's force can be felt. The solar wind pushes the magnetic field into a teardrop shape. This shape is called the planet's magneto- sphere. Earth's magnetosphere keeps the solar wind from reaching Earth's surface.

Particles in the solar wind can get trapped in Earth's magnetic field. They cause beautiful shapes of red, green, and blue to dance across the sky. This is called an aurora. Auroras form in the atmosphere near Earth's North and South Poles. In the North- ern Hemisphere, an aurora is called the Northern Lights, or aurora borealis. In the Southern Hemisphere it is called aurora australis, or the Southern Lights.

CHAPTER FOUR

SUNSPOTS

Since ancient times, people have noticed dark spots on the Sun's surface. The ancient Greeks and Chinese observed them. Historians believe the Aztecs in Mexico may have seen them, too. There is an Aztec story about a god with marks on his face. The marked face could be the Sun. We now call these dark areas sunspots.

European astronomers studied sunspots after the telescope was invented in the 1600s. English astronomer Thomas Harriot was the first to observe sunspots with a

The ancient Aztecs used the Sun to measure time and often depicted the Sun's face at the center of their annual calendars.

telescope, but he did not publish his discovery. The Italian astronomer Galileo wrote letters explaining that sunspots were dark spots on the surface of the Sun. Some astronomers refused to believe Galileo. They believed the Sun was a perfect creation of God and could not have spots. They said the sunspots had to be moons or planets going around the Sun.

Now scientists know that sunspots are areas that are cooler than the rest of the Sun's photosphere. The Sun's surface is usually 9,900° F (5,500° C), but sunspots are 7,000° F (4,000° C). Sunspots can be large or small. Big sunspots can be several times larger than Earth.

Sometimes there are many sunspots, and sometimes there are few. The number of sunspots goes through cycles. A sunspot cycle lasts about 11 years. It goes from almost no sunspots to more than

100 at a time. Then a new 11-year cycle starts as the number goes back to almost no sunspots. The time when there are the most sunspots is called the solar maximum. The time when there are the fewest sunspots is called the solar minimum.

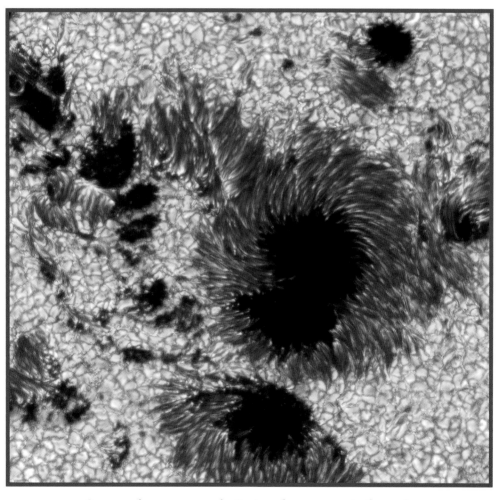

Sunspots that appear on the Sun's surface can remain for weeks,
but often they only last for a few days.

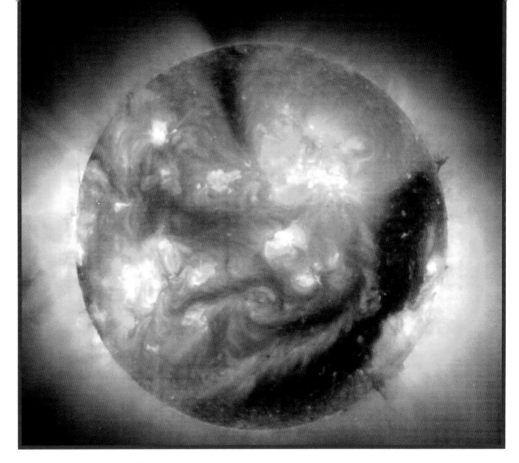

Using special filters on their equipment, astronomers are able to see sunspots as well as much of the Sun's other activity, which may affect Earth's weather.

It may be important to know when there will be many or fewer sunspots. Sunspots may affect Earth's weather. There were few sunspots between 1645 and 1715. This period is called the Little Ice Age because the temperatures on Earth were much colder than usual. But scientists have not proved there is a link between sunspots and weather on Earth.

CHAPTER FIVE

SOLAR STORMS

Sunspots are not the only areas of activity on the Sun. Hot gases leap up thousands of miles on the surface. Bright bursts of light called solar flares flash in the Sun's atmosphere. These kinds of violent activity are called solar storms.

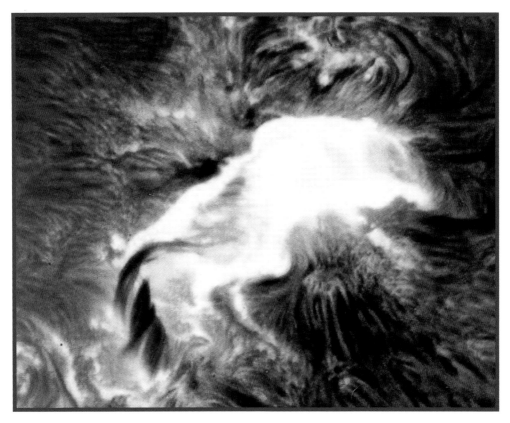

A single solar flare on the Sun can release more than a billion times as much energy as all the atomic bombs that have been exploded on Earth.

Solar storms are caused by the Sun's magnetism. The Sun acts as a powerful magnet. It is surrounded by a magnetic field, as are all magnets, but the Sun's magnetic field behaves strangely. It keeps changing. It weaves through the layers of the Sun. Sometimes it loops out of the Sun. Sometimes it streams off into space. Scientists do not completely understand the Sun's magnetic field.

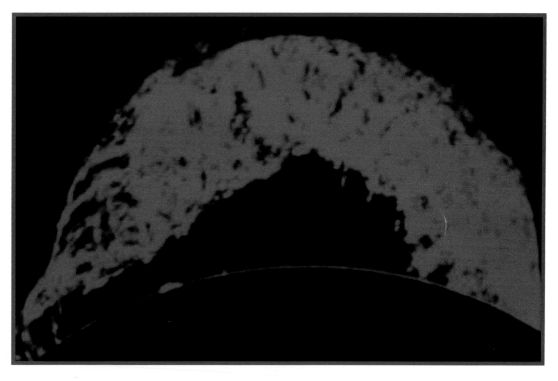

The strange behavior of the Sun's magnetic field is still mostly a mystery, but scientists do know that it is the cause of many of the Sun's unique characteristics, such as sunspots and solar storms.

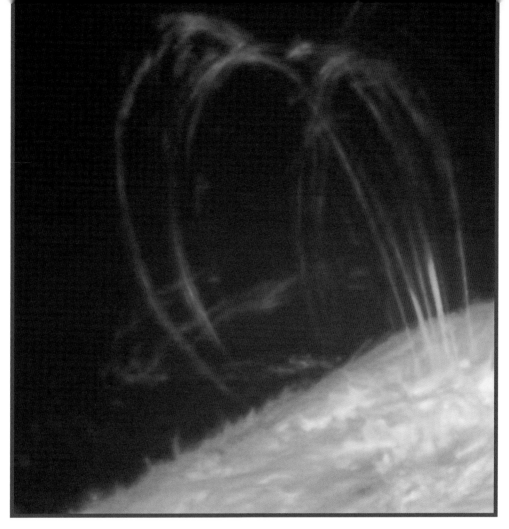

After a solar flare, solar loops appear above the surface of the Sun.

They do know that changes in the Sun's magnetic field cause

solar storms. Solar storms create magnetic storms on Earth.

Magnetic storms can cause power surges in electric power lines.

They can also cause problems with two-way radios. They some-

times damage man-made **satellites** and spacecraft.

Is there a link between storms on the Sun and the weather and climate on Earth? Scientists are pretty sure that the answer is yes. Teams of scientists from several countries are using information from spacecraft orbiting Earth and the Sun to explore the connection.

In 1994 and 1995, *Ulysses* became the first spacecraft to fly over the north and south poles of the Sun. It found that the fastest moving streams of gas in the solar wind come from the poles. *SOHO* has made important findings about sunspots and the Sun's jumping, twisting, and looping magnetic fields. Every day, cameras on *SOHO* send back amazing pictures of flaring gases for the scientists to study. Another project to study the Sun, called the Cluster project, launched four special satellites in 2000. They look for connections between what is happening on the Sun and what is happening in Earth's atmosphere.

Scientists want to learn how to predict "space weather." They want to know how changes in the number of sunspots affect the weather and climate on Earth. They are also studying how changes in the amount of light from the Sun affect Earth. Today, you listen to the regular weather forecast, which helps you know how to dress for the day. Someday, you may listen to the space weather forecast that helps you plan how to use your cell phone or the navigation system in your boat or car.

CHAPTER SIX

THE BIRTH AND DEATH OF THE SUN

The space between stars is filled with clouds of dust and gas.

Astronomers believe that the Sun formed from one of these

clouds. Gravity caused the particles of gas and dust to stick

together in the cloud.

Newer galaxies may begin to form in the clouds of dust and gas that stretch through space between the universe's already-existing galaxies. New stars are being born in this Doradus Nebula.

Like Earth's Sun, a star that formed from dust and gas millions of years ago, this group of young stars is going through the same process.

The Sun began as a spinning ball of gas in the center of that cloud. As the gas became more tightly packed, the center of the ball became very hot. When tiny bits of hydrogen gas, called atoms, got closer to each other, they started to join together. The Sun began to shine.

Nine planets and their moons formed from the dust and gas that was left around the Sun. The planets, pieces of rock called

asteroids, and icy comets all came from gas and dust in the cloud. Now, they all orbit the Sun.

Astronomers have studied many other stars to better understand the Sun. They use what they have learned about the Sun to better understand those stars.

When a star like our Sun begins to die, it loses energy and is stretched out by gravity to form something called a nebula. By studying the dying Ant Nebula, Astronomers hope to learn what the future may hold for Earth's Sun.

They have learned that stars go through stages. They have predicted what will happen to our Sun. Someday, the Sun will run out of fuel in its core. The outer layers of the Sun will expand and will be released into the solar system. Only the core will be left. This is called a "white dwarf." Over tens of billions of years, the white dwarf will cool off and become a black dwarf. But don't start worrying yet. Astronomers say that the Sun will keep shining for at least another five billion years!

Glossary

asteroids (ASS-tuh-royds) Asteroids are rocky objects that orbit the Sun.

astronomers (uh-STRAW-nuh-merz) Astronomers are scientists who study space and the stars and planets.

climate (KLYE-mit) The climate of a place is the kind of weather it normally has.

comet (KOM-it) A comet is a bright object followed by a tail of dust and ice that orbits the Sun in a long, oval-shaped path.

gravity (GRA-vi-tee) Gravity is a force that pulls one object toward another.

hemisphere (HEM-uhss-fihr) One half of a sphere, such as the northern half or southern half of Earth when it is divided in two by the equator, is called a hemisphere.

particles (PAR-tuh-kuhls) Particles are tiny pieces of something.

satellites (SAH-tuh-lites) Satellites are objects in orbit around a larger object in space, such as Earth, and can be man-made or natural. For example, the Moon is a natural satellite of Earth.

telescopes (TEL-uh-skopes) Telescopes are instruments used to study things that are far away, such as stars and planets, by making them seem larger and closer.

Did You Know?

▶ It takes light from the Sun about 8 minutes and 20 seconds to reach Earth. Light travels at 186,282 miles (299,792 km) per second. This is called the speed of light.

▶ Our Sun is not the biggest kind of star. Neither is it the smallest. The biggest stars are 1,000 times larger than the Sun. The smallest stars are 10 times smaller than the Sun. The Sun is a type of star called a yellow dwarf.

▶ We use many kinds of energy sources to make heat or electricity on Earth. Some sources are burning oil or moving water. Solar energy is a source that we get right directly sunlight. Energy from the Sun helps heat homes, light classrooms, and even run some cars!

▶ The Sun is so large that if you could place all of the solar system's planets, moons, comets, and asteroids inside, they would all fit, with room left over!

Fast Facts

Diameter: 864,000 miles (1.4 million km)

Atmosphere: hydrogen and helium

Time to orbit the galaxy: 200 million years

Time to turn on axis: 25.4 Earth-days

Average distance from Earth: about 93 million miles (150 million km)

Shortest distance from Earth: 91 million miles (146 million km)

Greatest distance from Earth: 94.5 million miles (152 million km)

Surface gravity: 28 times that of Earth. A person weighing 80 pounds (36 kg) on Earth would weigh about 2,244 pounds (1,018 kg) on the Sun's surface.

Surface temperature: 9,900° F (5,500° C)

Core temperature: 28,000,000° F (16,000,000° C)

How to Learn More about the Sun

At the Library

Barnes-Svarney, Patricia. *Secrets of the Sun: A Closer Look at Our Star.*
Austin, Tex.: Raintree Steck-Vaughn, 2000.

Goldstein, Margaret J. *The Sun.* Minneapolis: Lerner Publications, 2003.

Lassieur, Allison. *The Sun.* New York: Children's Press, 2000.

Prinja, Raman. *The Sun.* Chicago: Heinemann Library, 2002.

Schwabacher, Martin. *The Sun.* New York: Benchmark Books, 2003.

On the Web

Visit our home page for lots of links about the Sun:
http://www.childsworld.com/links.html
Note to Parents, Teachers, and Librarians: We routinely verify our Web links to
make sure they're safe, active sites—so encourage your readers to check them out!

Through the Mail or by Phone

ADLER PLANETARIUM AND ASTRONOMY MUSEUM
1300 South Lake Shore Drive
Chicago, IL 60605-2403
312/922-STAR

NATIONAL AIR AND SPACE MUSEUM
7th and Independence Avenue, S.W.
Washington, DC 20560
202/357-2700

ROSE CENTER FOR EARTH AND SPACE
AMERICAN MUSEUM OF NATURAL HISTORY
Central Park West at 79th Street
New York, NY 10024-5192
212/769-5100

The Sun

Mercury

Venus

Earth

Mars

Jupiter

Saturn

Uranus

Neptune

Pluto

The solar system

Index

animal life, 5
astronomers, 7, 13, 14, 18, 27
atmosphere, 13–14
auroras, 16
axis, 5
Aztecs, 17

Babylonians, 8
"black dwarfs," 27

Chinese, 17
chromosphere, 14
Cluster project, 24
convection zone, 10–11
core, 10, 27
corona, 14–15, 16

daytime, 6

Earth, 4, 5–6, 8, 10, 14, 16, 20, 23, 24
eclipse, 8, 14
Egyptians, 8

formation, 25–27

galaxies, 4

Galileo, 18
gravity, 4, 25
Greeks, 8, 17

Harriot, Thomas, 17–18
Helios, 8
helium, 9, 13
hydrogen, 9, 13, 26

Inca culture, 8

life, 4, 5
light rays, 10
Little Ice Age, 20

magnetic field, 16, 22–23
magnetic storms, 23
magnetism, 22
magnetosphere, 16
Maya culture, 8
Milky Way galaxy, 4

nighttime, 6
Northern Lights, 16

orbit, 4–5

photosphere, 11–12, 18

plant life, 5

radiation, 10
radiation zone, 10

Solar and Heliospheric Observatory (SOHO), 7, 14
solar flares, 21
solar maximum, 19
solar minimum, 19
solar storms, 21–23
solar wind, 15, 16
Southern Lights, 16
"space weather," 24
spacecraft, 7, 14, 23, 24
stars, 4
sunspot cycles, 18–19
sunspots, 17–20, 24
surface, 11, 17

telescopes, 7, 17, 18
temperatures, 10, 14, 18

Ulysses spacecraft, 24

"white dwarfs," 27

About the Author

Darlene R. Stille is a science writer. She has lived in Chicago, Illinois, all her life. When she was in high school, she fell in love with science. While attending the University of Illinois she discovered that she also loved writing. She was fortunate to find a career that allowed her to combine both her interests. Darlene Stille has written about 60 books for young people.